Kids Do Magic!

By Ruth Owen

WINDMILL
BOOKS

Published in 2017 by Windmill Books,
an Imprint of Rosen Publishing
29 East 21st Street, New York, NY 10010

First Edition

Produced for Windmill by Ruby Tuesday Books Ltd
Designer: Emma Randall

Photo Credits: Courtesy of Ruby Tuesday Books and Shutterstock.

Cataloging-in-Publication Data
Names: Owen, Ruth.
Title: Kids do magic! / Ruth Owen.
Description: New York : Windmill Books, 2017. | Series: Creative kids| Includes index.
Identifiers: ISBN 9781499481136 (pbk.) | ISBN 9781508192213 (library bound) |
    ISBN 9781508192091 (6 pack)
Subjects: LCSH: Magic tricks--Juvenile literature.
Classification: LCC GV1548 .O94 2017 | DDC 793.8--dc23

Manufactured in the United States of America
CPSIA Compliance Information: Batch #BS16PK: For Further Information contact
Windmill Books, New York, New York at 1-866-478-0556

Contents

Magician Words

- A magician has an **act**, which is a set of magic tricks that he or she performs.

- A magician is a performer, just like an actor or singer. As he or she performs a trick, a magician might tell a story, crack jokes, or explain to the audience what is happening. This is called a magician's **patter**.

- Some tricks use a **gimmick**. This is a piece of equipment or an effect that the audience doesn't see. Often a gimmick is set up in advance of doing a trick.

Get Creative with Magic

Do you love to watch magicians such as Penn and Teller, David Blaine, and Dynamo? Are you amazed by the tricks they perform? If so, there's no better time than now to get started on your own future career as a magician.

In the past, magicians mostly performed their acts in theaters or on stage in a TV studio. Today, magicians such as Dynamo perform incredible **close-up magic** on street corners and fans around the world can watch them on YouTube.

Think up a magician name for yourself and use it when you're performing.

Every famous magician got started by learning a few basic tricks like the ones in this book. Each trick is simple to learn, and with a little practice, you'll be wowing your friends and family.

"Abracadabra" is probably the most famous magic word, but why not make up your own unique magical word or phrase to use when you're doing a trick?

You Will Need:

• A pack of playing cards

Awesome Card Trick

As with all card tricks, make sure you practice before you perform this trick for an audience. It's easy to learn, though, and you'll soon be impressing your friends with your awesome magic skills!

1 To prepare the trick, place the cards in a stack facedown. Look at the top card and memorize it. For example, our card will be the seven of diamonds. Don't let your audience see you do this.

2 Begin your performance by placing the deck of cards facedown on a table. Ask an audience member to cut the cards and place the cut cards faceup on the table.

Cut cards placed faceup

3 Then place the cut cards back on the stack, still faceup.

4 Now ask the audience member to cut the cards again farther down the pack, and place the cut cards back on the stack faceup.

Faceup cards from stack

5 One by one, remove the faceup cards from the stack and place them to one side until you reach a card that is not faceup.

This card will be the seven of diamonds

The card that's facedown will be the one that was originally on the top of the stack (the seven of diamonds).

6 Without looking at the card that's facedown, hold it up and show the audience member.

This card is the seven of diamonds

Your patter:
Please memorize this card, but don't tell me what it is.

As the audience member is memorizing the card, study him carefully as if you are trying to read his mind!

7 Place the card back on the stack, facedown. Gather up the rest of the cards and place them facedown on top.

8 Now ask the audience member to shuffle the cards. Then place the stack facedown back on the table.

9 One by one, slowly turn over the cards. You know that you are looking for the seven of diamonds.

10 For effect, as you turn over the cards, every now and again, stop at a card and for just a few seconds look at the audience member as if you're trying to read his mind and you're considering if the card you're holding is his or not.

11 When the seven of diamonds appears, hold it up and say to your audience member:

Is this your card?
Your audience will be wowed!

You Will Need:

- A banana

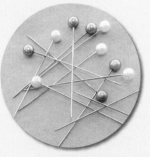

- A dressmaking pin

This trick requires some advance setup, but it's easy to do and will wow your friends!

1 Choose a banana that has a good pattern of light and dark patches. It will help to disguise your trickery!

2 About one third of the way along the banana, carefully push the pin into the banana.

3 Then wriggle the pin back and forth. You want to make the smallest pinprick in the skin, but inside the skin, the pin will be sawing through the soft banana.

4 Repeat in two more places. The trick is now ready to be performed.

Push in the pin in three places.

Inside the skin, the banana will be sliced in four. Your audience won't be able to see the pinpricks in the skin, though.

5 Present the banana to your audience. Tell them you are going to cut it into four pieces using only your magic powers.

6 Hold your hand above the banana and make a sawing motion in midair above one of the places where you cut the banana with the pin. Then repeat in the other two spots.

7 Carefully peel the banana and to the amazement of your audience, it will fall into four pieces.

You Will Need:

- A dollar bill

- 2 paper clips

This is a neat close-up magic trick that is great fun to perform.

1 Fold the dollar bill in two places along the dotted lines, as shown. The top edge of the dollar bill should form a Z shape.

2 Slide one paper clip over the back and center part of the dollar bill, as shown.

3 Slide the second paper clip over the center and front part of the dollar bill, as shown.

Make sure you practice positioning the paper clips before you perform this trick.

4 Now take hold of the two ends of the dollar bill.

Hold here

Hold here

Pull in this direction

Pull in this direction

5 Pull, or snap, the dollar bill and the paper clips will fly up into the air.

6 When the paper clips land on the ground, they will be linked together!

You Will Need:

- 2 small rectangles of colorful paper

- 1 sheet of white paper

- A glass

- A pencil

- Scissors

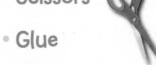

- Glue

- Tape

- A coin

1 To prepare the trick, stand the glass upside down on one of the pieces of colored paper. Draw around the rim of the glass.

2 Carefully cut out the circle of paper. Then glue the circle to the rim of the glass.

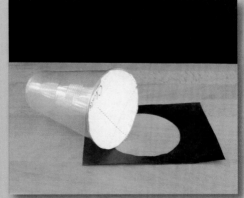

When the glass is upturned it should look like this.

3 Now make a tube from the white paper that fits snugly over the glass.

4 To set up the trick, before the audience is watching, place the second colored piece of paper on a tabletop.

5 On one side of the paper, place the glass upside down. The audience will think it is a normal, empty glass.

6 Next to the glass, place the coin. You are ready to begin.

7 Point to the items on the table, in turn.

Your patter:
Using magic and this glass, I am going to make the coin disappear.

8 Cover the glass with the paper tube.

9 Then pick up the glass and tube and place them on top of the coin.

As you speak, wave your hands over the glass.

Your patter:
The glass is now covering the coin. I will say the magic words....

10 Lift the tube from the glass.

Your patter:
Hey presto! The coin has disappeared.

(Of course, the coin is actually under the circle of paper that you glued to the rim of the glass.)

11 Put the paper tube back over the glass. Wave your hands over the glass and say your magic word again.

12 Then pick up the glass and tube and return them to their starting position. The coin will have magically reappeared!

As you perform the trick, be very careful to not let the audience see that the glass is really a gimmick that you prepared in advance.

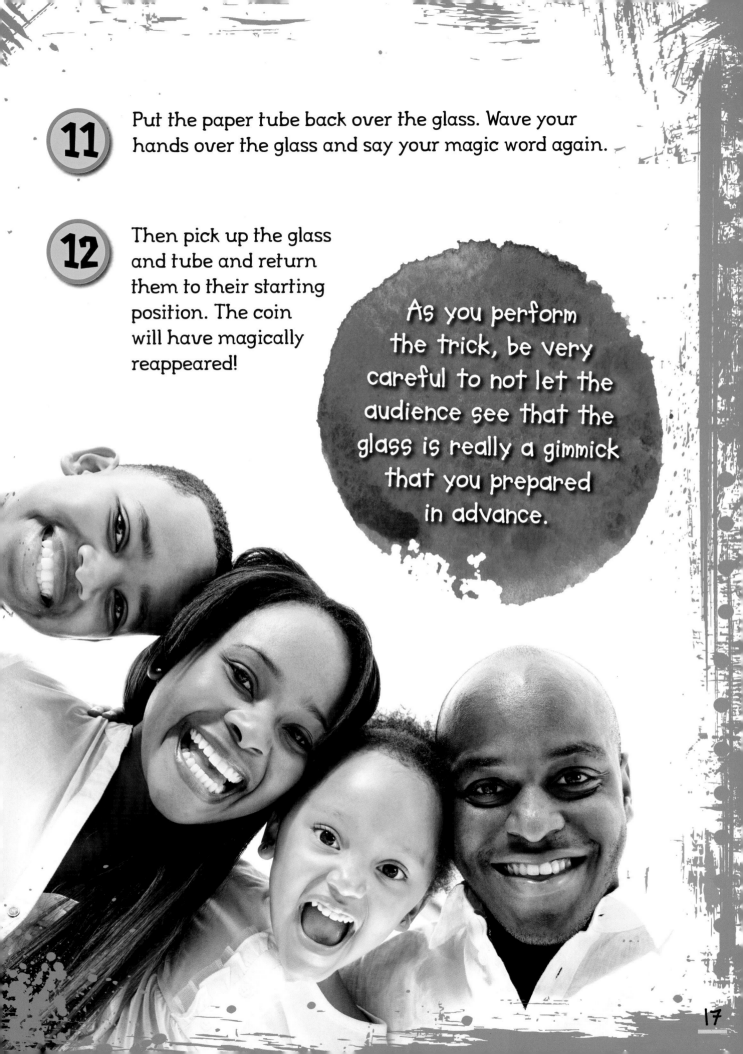

You Will Need:

- A pack of playing cards

Happy Royal Families Trick

As you perform this trick, you can tell a story to make it more enjoyable for your audience. Try using the story below, or make up your own version!

1 Take the 12 picture cards and the four aces from your pack. Group them into the four **suits** (hearts, diamonds, clubs, and spades) and lay them out as below.

Your patter:
There were once four royal families. Each family lived in their own castle. The families were miserable, though. The kings had no one to go hunting with. The queens had no one to chat and drink tea with. The young princes were bored because they wanted to do sports, and the baby princesses had no one to play with.

2 Gather up each set of four cards with the aces (the baby princesses) on the top of each set.

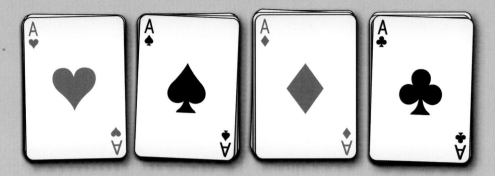

Then place the four sets on top of each other to make a single stack.

> *Your patter:*
> *So the four royal families got together to have a meeting.*

 3 Now place the stack of cards facedown.

4 Ask a member of the audience to cut the cards, by moving part of the stack to the right-hand side and then putting the left-hand stack on top.

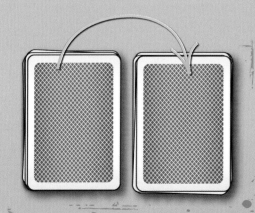

5 Ask the audience member to cut the cards again, repeating step 4.

Your patter:
The royal families talked and talked until they came up with a plan.

6 Pick up the stack and begin laying out the cards to form a square in a clockwise direction.

Lay this card first

Card 2

Card 4

Card 3

Your patter:
After the meeting, everyone went back to the four palaces.

7 Continue adding a single card to each of the four stacks, working around in a clockwise direction until all 16 cards are back on the table.

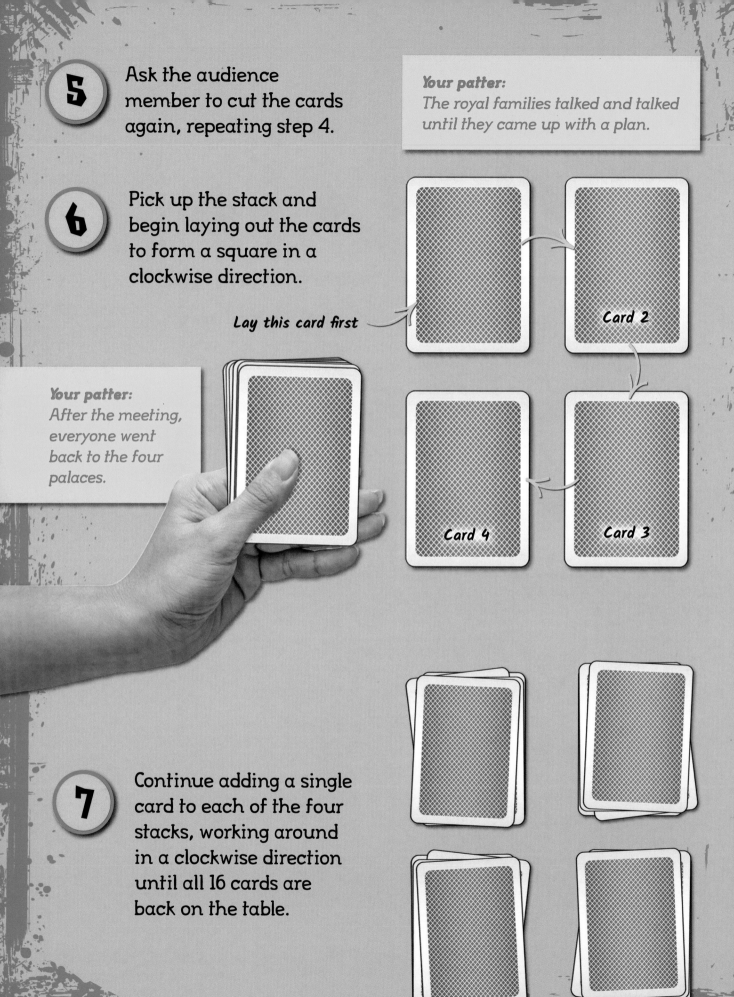

Now turn over stack 1.

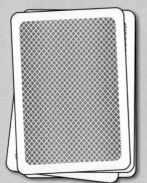

Your patter:
All the baby princesses went to one castle where they could play together.

9 Then turn over stacks 2, 3, and 4, and you will see that all the cards are now grouped as aces, jacks, queens, and kings.

Your patter:
All the kings lived in another castle and could go hunting together. The queens spent their days drinking tea and chatting, and the princes were finally able to play sports. And they all lived happily ever after!

You Will Need:

- A foil dish

- Water

- 7 toothpicks

- Clear dishwashing detergent

Your patter:
I am placing the toothpicks in the shape of a pentagon.

This trick uses science to create a great magic effect!

1 Before you perform this trick, you will need to prepare a toothpick. Dip the toothpick into the detergent. Allow any excess to drip off, so it's not obvious to your audience that the toothpick is different from the others.

2 To perform the trick, fill the foil dish with water to just below the rim.

3 Take five toothpicks and lay them on the surface of the water in the shape of a pentagon. The toothpicks' ends should cross over each other.

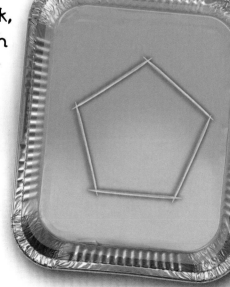

4 Hold up the toothpick that you dipped in detergent. Wave your other hand over the toothpick and say your magic word.

Your patter:
I have given this toothpick magic powers so it will be able to break the pentagon apart.

5 Dip the detergent-covered toothpick into the center of the pentagon and the five toothpicks will fly apart.

6 If an audience member doubts your magic powers, set up the pentagon again. Then give the doubter a fresh toothpick (with no detergent on it). When that person tries, nothing will happen!

If the audience wants you to repeat the trick, just say your magic powers need to take a little rest!

7 How does it work? This trick works because the detergent forces the water **molecules** apart. This breaks the **surface tension**, causing ripples that make the five toothpicks instantly move apart.

You Will Need:

- A small bowl

- Milk

- Black pepper

- Clear dishwashing detergent

Milk and Pepper Trick

Just like the toothpick trick on page 22, this trick uses dishwashing detergent to break the surface tension of a liquid and create a great "magical" effect.

1 To set up the trick, fill the bowl with milk to just below the rim.

2 Sprinkle a layer of black pepper onto the milk. The trick is now ready to perform.

3 Without your audience seeing, dip one of your fingers into some clear dishwashing detergent.

4 To begin your performance, dip a finger from your left hand into the milk. (Nothing will happen.)

Your patter:
Observe how I'm dipping my finger into the milk and pepper.

 5 Now hold up the finger that you dipped in dishwashing detergent. (Make sure your audience can't see the detergent.)

Your patter:
I'm now going to use magic to make the pepper swim across the milk.

Say your magic word.

 6 Dip your finger into the milk and the pepper will fly to the sides of the bowl!

If anyone in your audience doesn't believe you've used magic, set up the trick again and ask them to see if they can move the pepper!

You Will Need:

- One sheet of printer paper

- A pair of scissors

This is a fun trick that will have your friends howling with frustration when they realize how easily you've tricked them!

1 Show your friend or audience member the sheet of paper.

Your patter:
I bet you that I can cut a hole in this piece of paper that's big enough for me to step through.

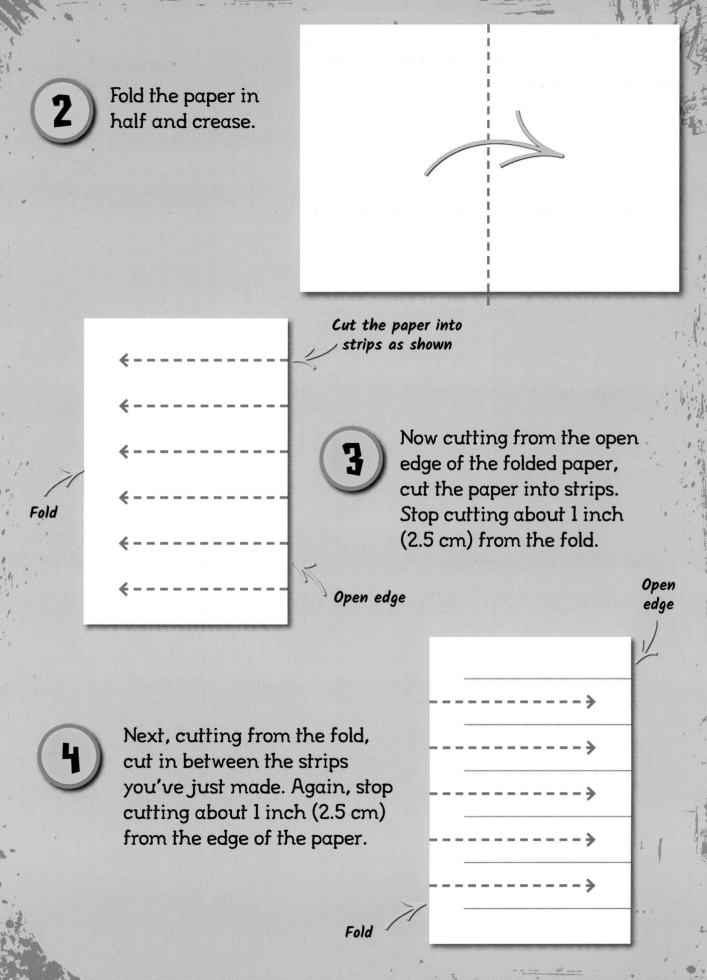

2 Fold the paper in half and crease.

Cut the paper into strips as shown

Fold

Open edge

3 Now cutting from the open edge of the folded paper, cut the paper into strips. Stop cutting about 1 inch (2.5 cm) from the fold.

Open edge

4 Next, cutting from the fold, cut in between the strips you've just made. Again, stop cutting about 1 inch (2.5 cm) from the edge of the paper.

Fold

5

Finally, cut through the ends of the strips where there is a fold. But don't cut the two end strips.

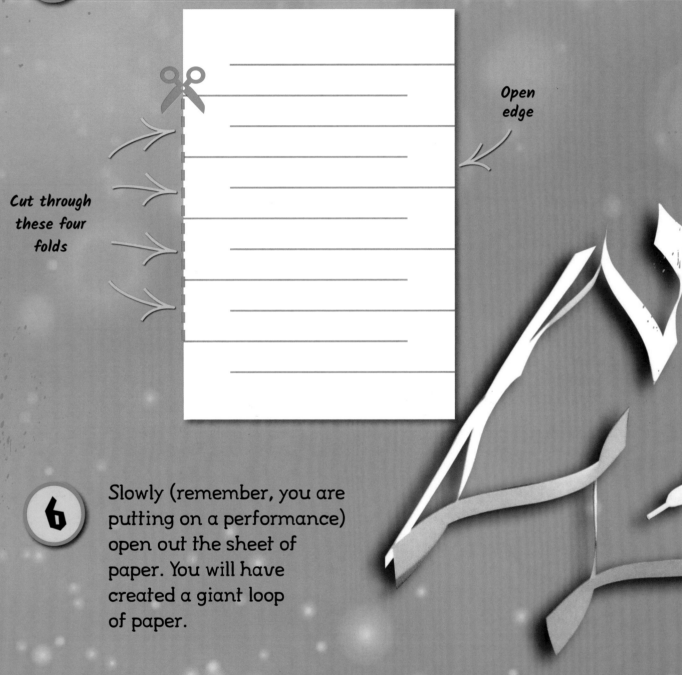

Open edge

Cut through these four folds

6

Slowly (remember, you are putting on a performance) open out the sheet of paper. You will have created a giant loop of paper.

Your patter:
As you can see, I have a cut a hole in this piece of paper that is big enough for me to step through!

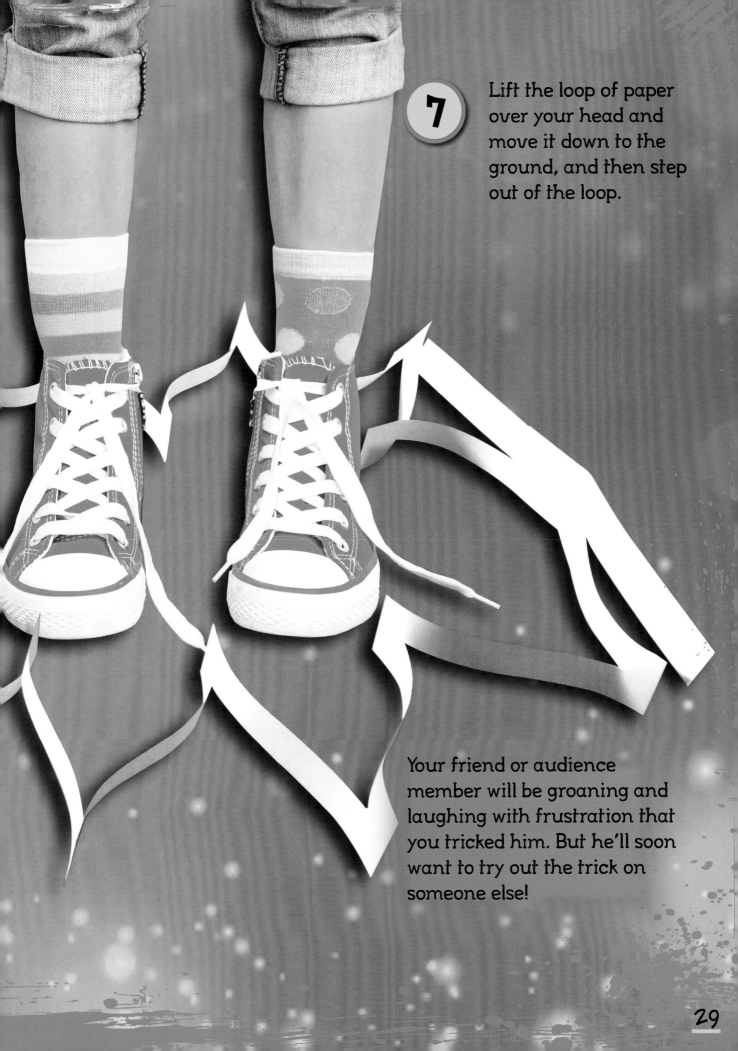

7 Lift the loop of paper over your head and move it down to the ground, and then step out of the loop.

Your friend or audience member will be groaning and laughing with frustration that you tricked him. But he'll soon want to try out the trick on someone else!

Glossary

act
In the world of magic, a collection of magic tricks performed regularly by a magician along with any patter.

close-up magic
Magic that is performed sitting or standing just a few feet from your audience.

gimmick
The sneaky part of a trick that the audience doesn't see. For example, a piece of equipment that has been changed or set up in some way in advance that allows a trick to work.

molecules
Small parts of something made from two or more atoms. For example, a water molecule is made of two atoms of hydrogen and one atom of oxygen.

patter
The words spoken by a magician as he or she is performing a trick. Patter can be a story, an explanation, or a joke.

suits
The four sets (diamonds, hearts, spades, and clubs) that playing cards are divided into.

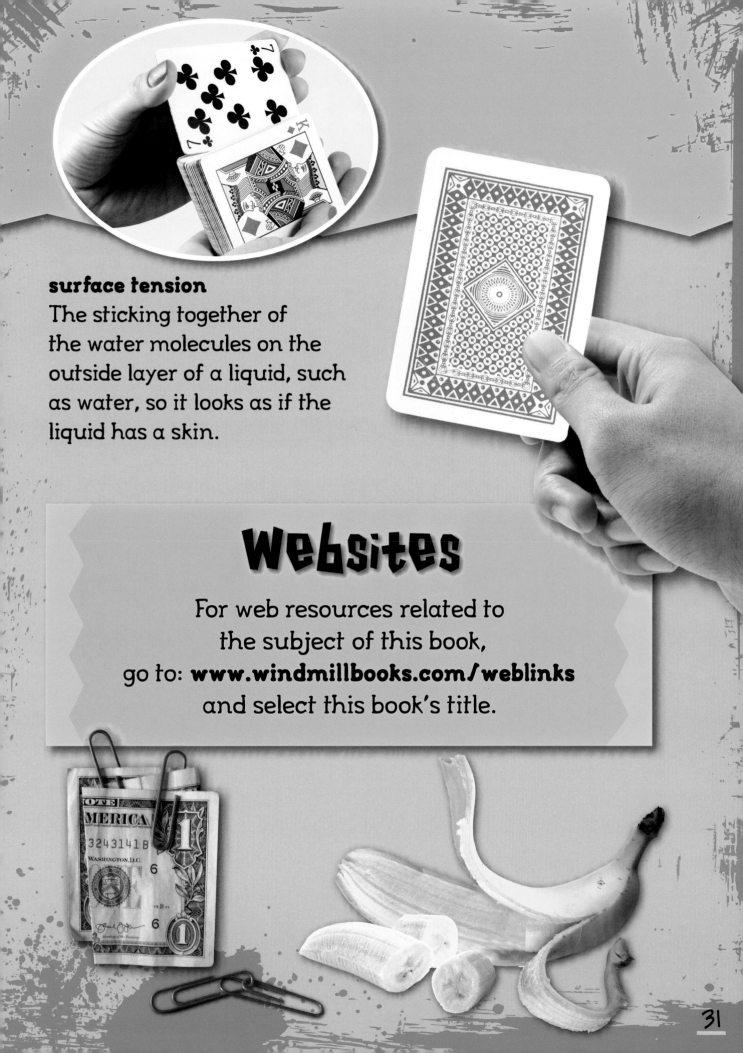

surface tension
The sticking together of
the water molecules on the
outside layer of a liquid, such
as water, so it looks as if the
liquid has a skin.

Websites

For web resources related to
the subject of this book,
go to: **www.windmillbooks.com/weblinks**
and select this book's title.

Index